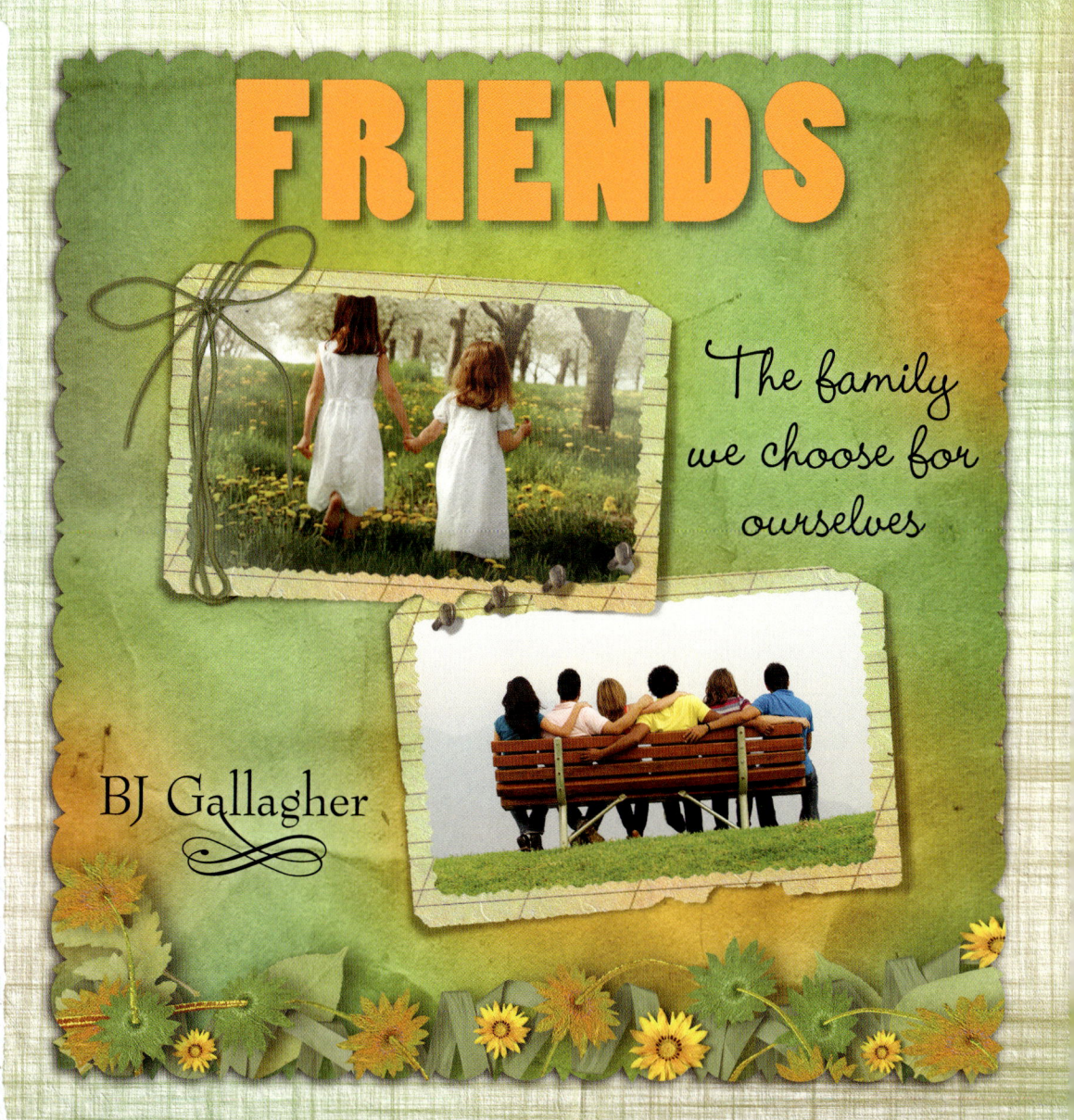

Copyright © 2011 by BJ Gallagher

Published by Simple Truths, LLC
1952 McDowell Road, Suite 300
Naperville, Illinois 60563
800-900-3427

All rights reserved. No portion of this book may be reproduced, stored in a retrieval system or transmitted in any form by any means—except for brief quotations in printed reviews—without the prior written permission of the publisher.

Simple Truths is a registered trademark.

Design: Simple Truths designer Lynn Harker
Photos: ThinkStock and ShutterStock

Printed and bound in the United States of America

WOZ 10 9 8 7 6 5 4 3 2

Dedication

My life and my heart are filled with the gifts my friends have given me—gifts of time, gifts of listening and caring, gifts of encouragement and support, gifts of love and laughter. This book is my thank-you gift to all my wonderful friends— with love, gratitude, and deep appreciation.

A True Friend...

Accepts you, just as you are. 6

Believes in your potential. 10

Comforts you when you're sad. 16

Delights in your successes. 20

Empathizes with your struggles. 26

Forgives you when you hurt her feelings, just as you do for her. 30

Gives you time and attention. 34

Hugs you ... often. 38

Inspires you to do your best. 42

Just loves you. 46

Keeps your secrets. 50

Listens with her heart. 54

Makes you want to be a better person. 58

NEVER judges you. 62
OCCASIONALLY disappoints you 'cause she's human, too. 68
POINTS out your good qualities when you forget. 72
QUESTIONS you when you're about to do something really dumb. 76
RESPECTS your boundaries. 80
SHARES her hopes and fears with you. 86
TELLS you the truth. 90
UNDERSTANDS you, even when you don't understand yourself. 94
VALUES your ideas and opinions. 100
WILL DO anything she can to help you. 106
XTENDS the benefit of the doubt to you. 110
YEARNS to hear from you when you're away. 114
ZINGS with joy 'cause you're friends. 118
The friendship promise 122

A True Friend...

Accepts you, just as you are.

A friend is someone who understands your past, believes in your future, and accepts you just the way you are.

ANONYMOUS

Truth in Advertising

"As is" the sign reads
    in the window of the used car.

"That's me,"
    I think.

My friends see my dings and dents,
    my less than perfect paint,
        the subtle signs of wear and tear,
    and they know that I am far from perfect.

But they take me anyway,
    just the way I am.

≈ AS IS. ≈

True Friendships are UNCONDITIONAL...

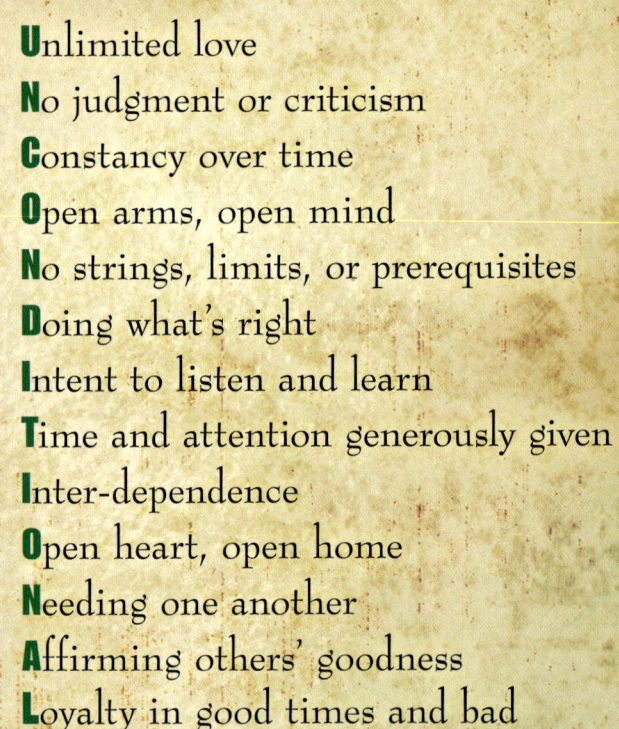

Unlimited love
No judgment or criticism
Constancy over time
Open arms, open mind
No strings, limits, or prerequisites
Doing what's right
Intent to listen and learn
Time and attention generously given
Inter-dependence
Open heart, open home
Needing one another
Affirming others' goodness
Loyalty in good times and bad

No Strings Attached

No strings attached,
   no terms and conditions,
      no hesitation or reservations …
that's how you love me.

You embrace me just as I am,
   and I do the same for you.

Mutual trust and respect,
   unconditional love and acceptance,
      commitment to each other's wellbeing …
that's what we have.

      In other words,
         we're true friends.

A True Friend...

Believes in your potential.

A friend is someone who knows the song in your heart and can sing it back to you when you have forgotten the words.

ANONYMOUS

I've learned that people will forget what you said; people will forget what you did; but people will never forget how you made them feel.

— Maya Angelou

The glory of friendship is not in the outstretched hand, nor the kindly smile, nor the joy of companionship; it is in the spiritual inspiration that comes to one when he discovers that someone else believes in him and is willing to trust him with his friendship!

— Ralph Waldo Emerson

'Atta Girl!

It's so easy for women
    to slip into self-doubt
        and feeling inadequate.
After all,
we shoulder a lot of responsibilities —
    being supportive of our mates,
    nurturing our children,
    staying in touch with extended family,
    holding down jobs
    while holding down the fort at home.

No wonder we sometimes feel
    anxious,
        exhausted,
            insecure,
                second guessing ourselves.

We need to know
    we're not alone.

We need to hear
    that other women
share our experiences.

"Atta girl" never sounded so sweet
    as when coming from the lips
        of another woman.
She understands,
    she's been there, done that.
She gets it –
    she gets *me.*

We take turns
    encouraging,
        supporting,
            cheering one another on.

We learn to do it for ourselves, too.
Just reach right over your shoulder, girl,
    and pat yourself on the back.

You're terrific,
    and you and I both know it.

CHEERING ME ON

"You can do it,"
 one friend says.

"Yes, it's a stretch,
but go for it anyway,"
 another urges.

"You're so talented—
I've always admired you,"
 still another joins in.

My friends are cheerleaders—
 a chorus of possibility.

Their words of **encouragement**
     compete in my mind
          with the sirens of self-doubt
               who sing songs of defeat and despair.

Who do I listen to?

The cheerleaders.

LOUDER please, girls,

I'm feeling a little shaky today.

A True Friend...

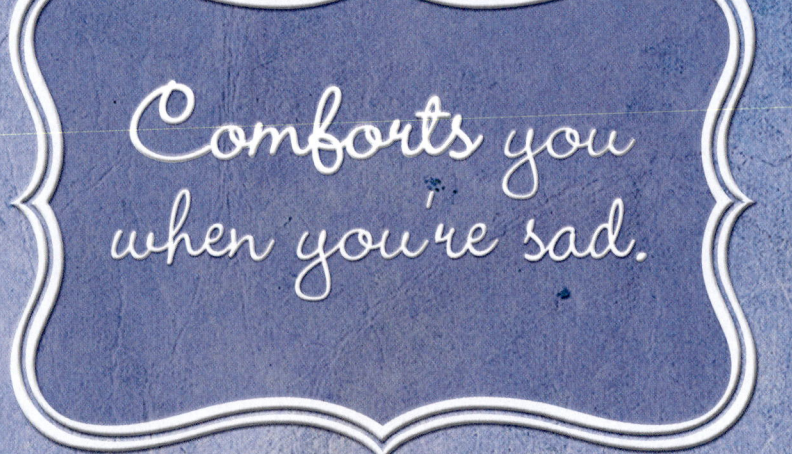

Comforts you when you're sad.

When we honestly ask ourselves which person in our lives means the most to us, we often find that it is those who, instead of giving advice, solutions, or cures, have chosen rather to share our pain and touch our wounds with a warm and tender hand. The friend who can be silent with us in a moment of despair or confusion, who can stay with us in an hour of grief and bereavement, who can tolerate not knowing, not curing, not healing and face with us the reality of our powerlessness, that is a friend who cares.

Henri Nouwen

That Which is Shareable is Bearable

I've learned that
   if I can share my troubles,
      I can bear them.

It's true.
It makes me feel better to have you around
   when I'm down.
Your presence reassures me;
   your listening soothes me;
      your hug consoles me.

      It's nice to have company —
         even if it's in the pits.

I don't need cheery platitudes of positive thinking
   or booming bravado urging me to "buck up."

No …
      What I really need right now
      is just the comfort of your company…

and maybe a little chocolate.

True friends provide COMFORT...

Caring companionship
Open arms
Much love
Food that nourishes and soothes
On-going support
Really good listening
Trust and confidence

Lots of people want to ride with you in the limo, but what you want is someone who will take the bus with you when the limo breaks down.

Oprah Winfrey

A True Friend...

Delights in your successes.

Life is partly what we make it,

and partly what it is made by the friends we choose.

TENNESSEE WILLIAMS

A True Friend Knows the Value of LAUGHTER...

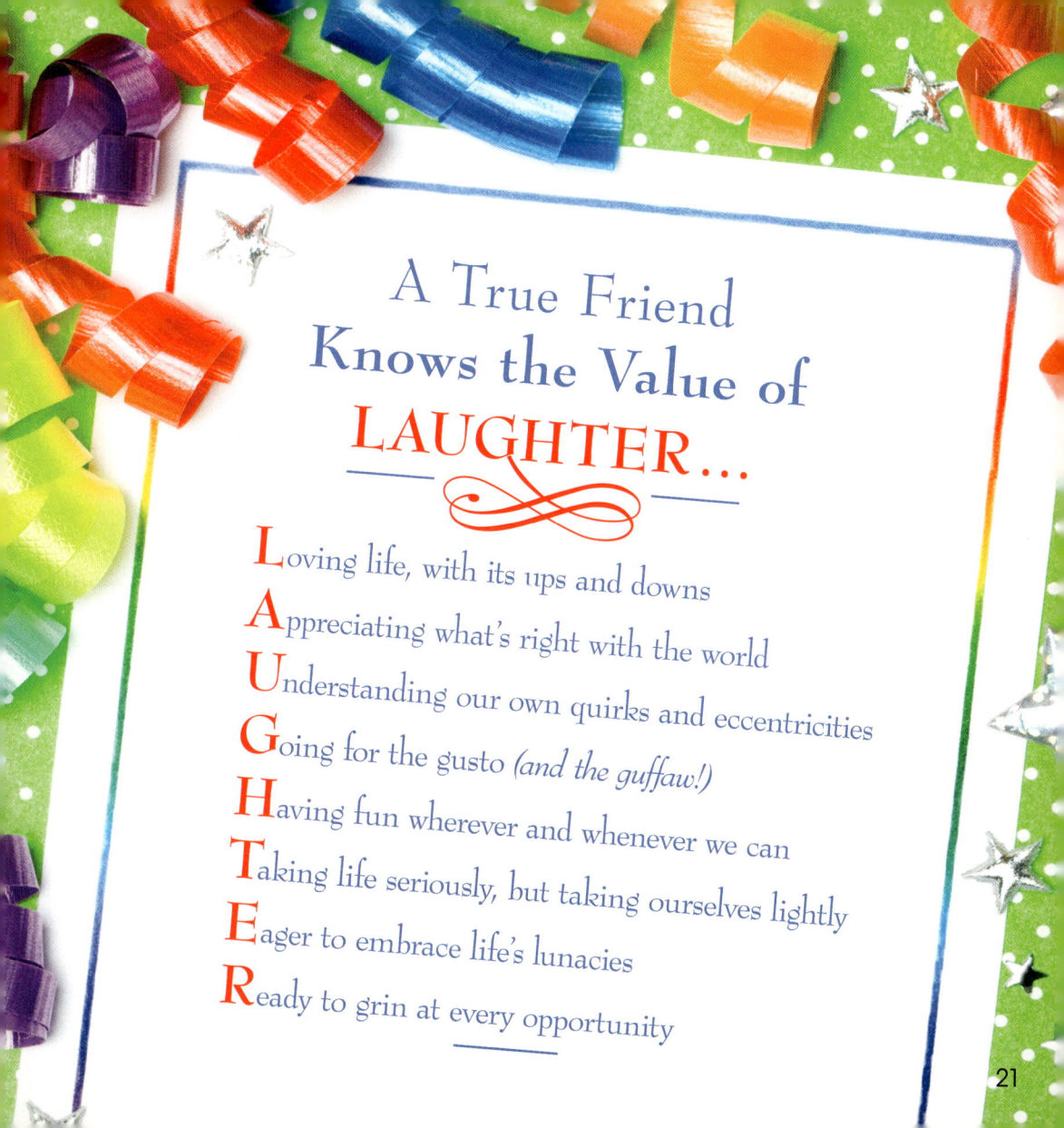

Loving life, with its ups and downs
Appreciating what's right with the world
Understanding our own quirks and eccentricities
Going for the gusto *(and the guffaw!)*
Having fun wherever and whenever we can
Taking life seriously, but taking ourselves lightly
Eager to embrace life's lunacies
Ready to grin at every opportunity

An ALL-WEATHER friend

It's easy to be my friend
when I'm having a hard time,
not doing so well.

Some friends hold out a helping hand,
offer me tea
with a bit of advice
and deep down inside
feel just a teensy little bit superior.
But those foul-weather friends
disappear like clouds
when my fortunes improve.

But you're here
in foul weather
and fair.
You delight when I'm on top of the world,
flying high,
reveling in success.

Your big smile says,
"Atta girl!
Way to go!"

You know that my achievement
doesn't diminish yours
and there's plenty of success
to go around.

CELEBRATE

"Good news!"

you announce happily
when I answer the phone.

"I got the promotion!"

We squeal excitedly
like a couple of schoolgirls.

"Where shall we go to celebrate?"

I ask.

"Pizza and beer
or steak and champagne?
You choose.
I'm buying!"

I'm as happy as if it was I
who got promoted.

For joy multiplies
    when it's shared.

And next time perhaps
    it will be me with the good news.

"Woo hoo! I landed the book deal!"

    I'll fire off in an e-mail to you.

A zillion happy faces
    will come back in your cyber reply.

"Celebrate?" you write.
"This time, I'm buying."

    "You bet,"
        I'll type back.

"How about Friday?"

That's the whole reason
to have good news,
    isn't it?
So we can celebrate
    with a true friend.

A True Friend...

Empathizes with your struggles.

Friendship is born at that moment when one person says to another, "What! You too? I thought I was the only one!"

C. S. LEWIS

Pain-full

I know you can't feel my pain,
  no one can.
My suffering is unique,
  as is yours and everyone else's too.

But it helps to know
  that you can imagine my pain
    as I struggle with this problem.
It helps to know that you've struggled, too,
  though our struggles may not be the same.

Thank you, Sister Struggler.
I can't feel your pain
  but I can feel your love.

This is my wish for you:

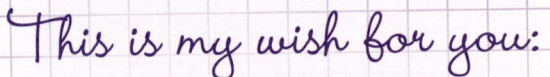

Comfort on difficult days,
Smiles when sadness intrudes,
Rainbows to follow the clouds,
Laughter to kiss your lips,
Sunsets to warm your heart,
Hugs when spirits sag,
Beauty for your eyes to see,
Friendships to brighten your being,
Faith so that you can believe,
Confidence for when you doubt,
Courage to know yourself,
Patience to accept the truth,
Love to complete your life.

anonymous

A True Friend...

Forgives you when you hurt her feelings, just as you do for her.

There is no love without forgiveness,
and there is no forgiveness without love.

BRYANT H. MCGILL

Mea Culpa

That old song is true:
"You often hurt
   the ones you love."

The careless comment,
   the commitment not kept,
     the promise broken.
I feel guilt, sadness,
   disappointment in myself.

Please forgive me—
   I didn't mean to hurt you.
How could I have done such a dumb thing?

You sigh and nod
   as you look at me with loving eyes.
Your hug tells me that you understand.
We smile at each other,
   wiping away a tender tear.

And we move on…

Until next time,
   when perhaps it's my turn
     to sigh and forgive.

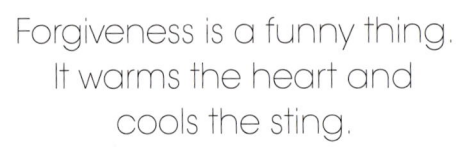

Forgiveness is a funny thing.
It warms the heart and
cools the sting.

WILLIAM ARTHUR WARD

Forgiveness does not
change the past, but it
does enlarge the future.

PAUL BOESE

To forgive is to set a prisoner
free and discover that the
prisoner was you.

LEWIS SMEDES

True Friends Extend
FORGIVENESS...

Feel your hurt

Open your mind

Release your anger

Give love a chance

Inquire within your heart

Venture into dialogue

Embrace the other person

Nudge yourself to keep at it, even when you don't want to

Enjoy new possibilities and freedom

Seek Divine guidance and help

Savor your new serenity and peace

A True Friend...

Gives you time and attention.

Friendship isn't a big thing ...
it's a million little things.

ANONYMOUS

Interest Compounded Daily

Our friendship
is like a bank account —
    growing in proportion
    to the amount of interest we pay.

A mutual fund,
we might call it —
    both of us enriched
    by our investment
    in one another.

Our assets include:
    compassion and caring,
      love and laughter,
        giving and gratitude.
We are wealthy
    beyond our wildest dreams.
We know that
    the best things in Life
        aren't things.

It only takes one smile to offer welcome …
    and blessed be the person who will share it.

It only takes one moment to be helpful …
    and blessed be the person who will spare it.

It only takes one joy to lift a spirit …
    and blessed be the person who will give it.

It only takes one life to make a difference …
    and blessed be the person who will live it.

Celebrate the happiness that friends are always giving …
    Make every day a holiday and celebrate just living!

AMANDA BRADLEY

True Friends Are Generous...

Giving with no strings attached

Expecting nothing in return

Noticing what others need and want

Exercising your imagination and creativity in giving

Realizing that "what goes around, comes around"

Opening your home as well as your heart

Understanding that it is the giver who is most enriched

Sharing your time, attention, energy, money and love

A True Friend...

Hugs you... often.

If you're alone, I'll be your shadow.
If you want to cry, I'll be your shoulder.
If you want a hug, I'll be your pillow.
If you need to be happy, I'll be your smile.
But anytime you need a friend, I'll just be me.

~ ANONYMOUS

A Call To Arms

Hug therapy ...

Safe,
inexpensive,
readily available,
needs no instruction manual,
proven effective,
guaranteed to lift spirits
and warm the heart.

I'm having new business cards printed:

"Hug Therapist"

You can't wrap love in a box, but you can wrap a person in a hug.

ANONYMOUS

A hug is like a boomerang ... you get it back right away.

BIL KEANE

Hugs Unlimited

How do I hug thee?
Let me count the ways ... *

- a happy hug when I meet you for lunch
- a comforting hug when you're sad or upset
- a congratulatory hug on your latest success
- a joyful hug when we get together for the holidays
- a birthday hug on your special day
- a "good-bye for now" hug whenever we part
- a happy surprise hug when we bump into each other unexpectedly

... and the list goes on.

Because, you know,
It's impossible to have too many hugs.

* with a grateful nod to Elizabeth Barrett Browning

A True Friend...

Inspires you to do your best.

One doesn't know, 'til one is a bit at odds with the world, how much one's friends who believe in one rather generously, mean to one.

D. H. LAWRENCE

Score: Love/Love

I've been told that
it's good to play tennis
with a partner who's better than you.
It improves your game
    and makes you play your best.

I feel that way
    about us.
Having you as my friend
    makes me do my best
        to rise to any occasion.

In our game of friendship
there are no losers –
    It's always win/win.

The greatest good you can do for another is not just to share your riches but to reveal to him his own.

BENJAMIN DISRAELI

My best friend is the one who brings out the best in me.

HENRY FORD

GOAL!

You're such a good influence on me.

You're like my coach,
 my cheerleader,
  my marching band
all rolled into one person.

Your confidence in me
 gives me confidence in me.

I can never fail
 with you in my corner.
I go for the goal
 'cause you've got my back.
I give it all I've got
 because you would expect
 nothing less.

Having you as my friend
 makes me a winner.

A True Friend...

Just Loves You.

What is a friend?
A single soul dwelling in two bodies.

ARISTOTLE

Grace-full

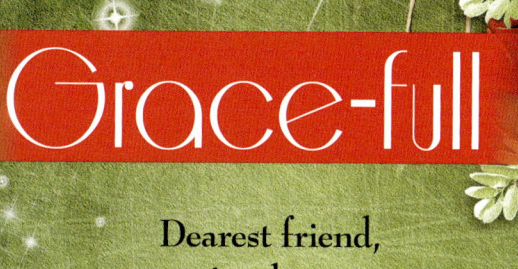

Dearest friend,
you've shown me
that you love me
not for what I do—
 but for who I am.

You've taught me that
I'm not a human doing—
 I'm a human being.

Your friendship isn't earned—
 it's a gift,
  freely given.

I'm deeply grateful …
 and grace-full.

Thank you.

To the world you may be just one person,
but to one person you may be the world.

Brandi Snyder

A friend is someone with whom
you dare to be yourself.

Frank Crane

A true friend knows how to **Love** ...

Laughs with you, not at you

Opens her heart, her arms, and her home

Voices her affection and appreciation

Embraces you with unconditional acceptance

A True Friend...

Keeps your secrets.

Friends are like bras: close to your heart and there for support.

ANONYMOUS

FRIENDSHIP CONFIDENTIAL

Some things are too important,
    too sensitive,
        too painful,
           too delicate
to be shared with the whole world.

Dreams,
    Hopes,
        Fears,
Memories,
    Fantasies,
        Heart's desires…
These are soul secrets,
    sacred trusts—
safe only with a bosom buddy
who will hold them gently
with love and respect
    in the confines of her own heart.

Thank you for being my confidante,
    my trusted friend,
        my secret agent.

What is love?

Love is when one person knows all of your secrets—your deepest, darkest, most dreadful secrets of which no one else in the world knows—and yet in the end, that one person does not think any less of you; even if the rest of the world does.

Anonymous

A friend is a person with whom I may be sincere. Before him, I may think aloud.

Ralph Waldo Emerson

A true friend knows how to

keep a SECRET...

Seals her lips

Engages in no gossip

Commits to confidentiality

Relays confidences to no one

Expressly promises to keep mum

Trusts that the secret is safe

A True Friend...

Listens with her heart.

The first duty of love is to listen.

PAUL TILLICH

Heart Sounds

Someone wise once told me,
 "The greatest gift
  you can give someone
  is the gift of the interested listener."

But no one had to tell you that ...
 you already knew.

Dearest friend,
you listen not just with your ears ...
but with your heart,
 your mind,
  your soul,
   your entire being.

You listen between the lines –
 paying attention
 to what I don't say,
  as well as what I do.

You genuinely want to know
 what's going on with me.

You listen
 to the language
 of my heart.

Deep listening is miraculous for both listener and speaker. When someone receives us with open-hearted, non-judging, intensely interested listening, our spirits expand.

Sue Patton Thoele

Listening is a magnetic and strange thing, a creative force. The friends who listen to us are the ones we move toward. When we are listened to, it creates us, makes us unfold and expand.

Karl A. Menninger

True friends know how to **LISTEN** ...

Lean in to establish rapport.

Interpret feelings as well as words.

Stay connected through eye contact.

Tune in to what's not being said as well as what is.

Express empathy and understanding.

Never interrupt, criticize, or judge ... **just LISTEN.**

A True Friend...

Makes you want to be a better person.

A friend accepts us as we are yet helps us to be what we should.

ANONYMOUS

Personal Best

I don't compete with you—
  I compete with myself.

But you play an important role—
  inspiring me,
    motivating me,
      being a great example.

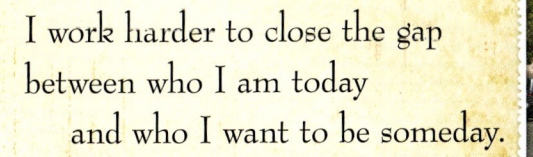

I work harder to close the gap
between who I am today
  and who I want to be someday.

Your love and support
help fuel my quest
  to achieve my personal best in Life.

If they ever held
an Olympic competition for friendships,
  ours would win the gold for sure!

No young man starting in life could have better capital than plenty of friends. They will strengthen his credit, support him in every great effort, and make him what, unaided, he could never be. Friends of the right sort will help him more—to be happy and successful—than much money …

Orison Swett Marden

Some people think only intellect counts: knowing how to solve problems, knowing how to get by, knowing how to identify an advantage and seize it. But the functions of intellect are insufficient without courage, love, friendship, compassion and empathy.

Dean Koontz

Inspired Friendship

You make me want to be
a better person –
    more thoughtful,
    more patient,
    more compassionate.

You inspire me,
    not with scolds or lectures,
but with the quiet example
    you set.

I look up to you;
    I respect you;
        I admire your gifts and your grace.

I love the way you walk your talk
    and live your beliefs.

Your integrity,
    character,
        and authenticity
make me grateful
that you're my friend.

I want to be just like you,
    when I grow up.

A True Friend...

Never judges you.

A true friend is someone who thinks that you're a good egg even though he knows that you are slightly cracked.

BERNARD MELTZER

True friends practice ACCEPTANCE...

Acknowledging the whole person
Coming to terms with flaws and failings
Committing to unconditional love
Entirely ignoring little things that really don't matter
Praising others' positive qualities
Taking time to listen patiently
Agreeing to mutual respect
Never trying to change others
Caring concern in all situations
Expressing appreciation

Juris Prudence

Judgments and opinions
are all around me —
some spoken,
some silent,
but nonetheless evident
in a frown,
   a shrug,
      a sigh,
a raised eyebrow,
   a barely audible "tch-tch."

My life is full of judges and juries.

Thankfully,
    you're not one of them.

To what do I owe
    your absence of evaluation and criticism?
How can I explain
    your unconditional positive regard—
        your complete acceptance of me as I am?

What say ye,
    ladies and gentlemen of the jury?

Motive: Love
Opportunity: Plenty
Verdict: Innocent of any crime
Sentence: A lifetime of friendship

~ The most I can do for my friend is simply
to be his friend. I have no wealth to bestow on him.
If he knows that I am happy in loving him,
he will want no other reward.
Is not friendship divine in this?

HENRY DAVID THOREAU ~

We need people in our lives with whom we can be as open as possible. To have real conversations with people may seem like such a simple, obvious suggestion, but it involves courage and risk.

THOMAS MOORE

A True Friend...

Occasionally disappoints you 'cause she's human, too.

It is one of the blessings of old friends that you can afford to be stupid with them.

RALPH WALDO EMERSON

PERFECTLY IMPERFECT

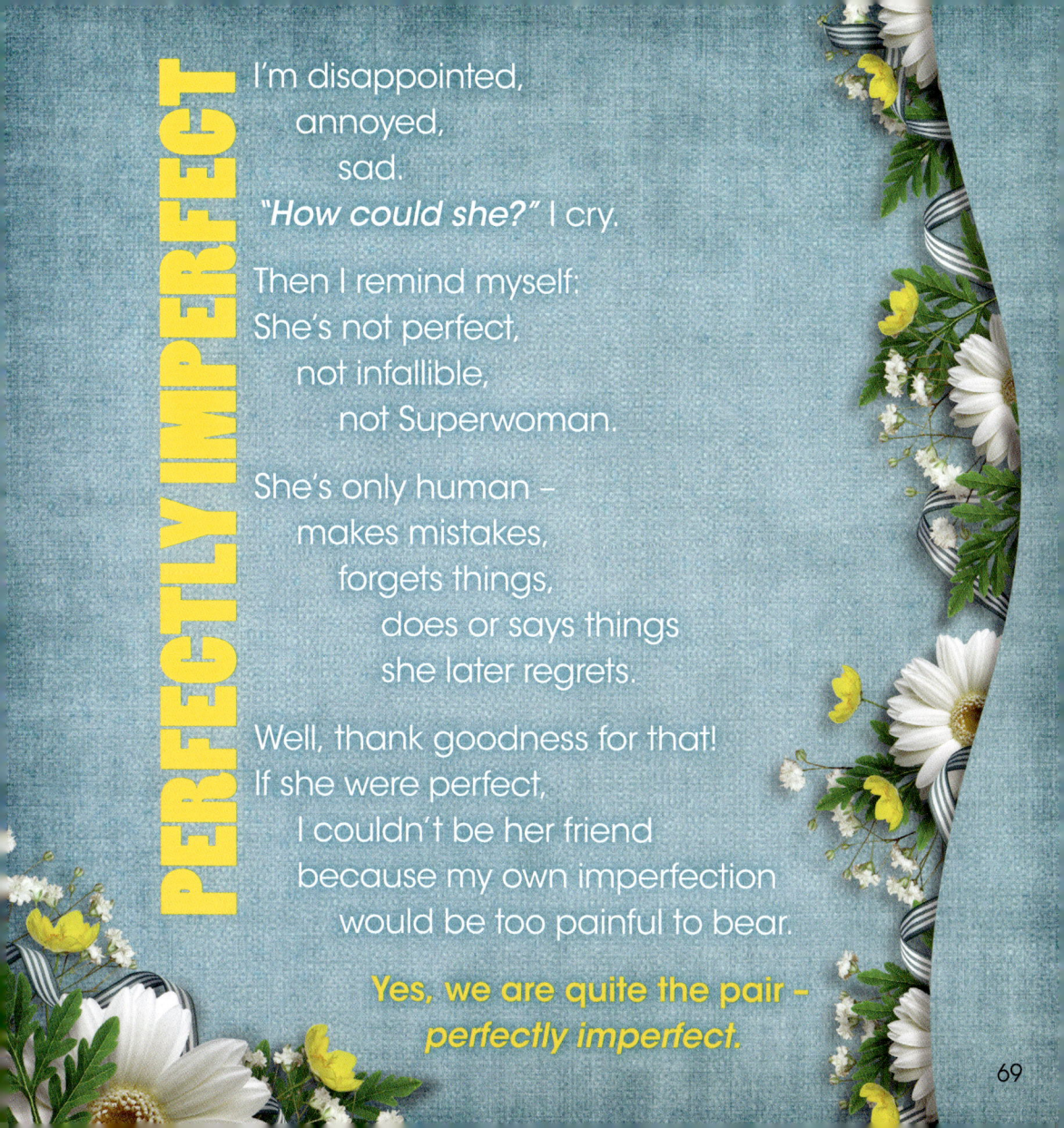

I'm disappointed,
   annoyed,
      sad.
"How could she?" I cry.

Then I remind myself:
She's not perfect,
   not infallible,
      not Superwoman.

She's only human –
   makes mistakes,
      forgets things,
         does or says things
           she later regrets.

Well, thank goodness for that!
If she were perfect,
   I couldn't be her friend
      because my own imperfection
         would be too painful to bear.

**Yes, we are quite the pair –
*perfectly imperfect.***

EXPECTATIONS

Someone wise once told me
that expectations are simply
    resentments waiting to happen.

I've learned the hard way
    how true this is.

A friend disappoints me
    and I'm hurt and angry.
Resentment bubbles up inside
    and I have a bitter taste in my mouth.
I want to complain and protest
    the disappointment I've suffered.

So, how long do I carry
my disappointment and resentment?

Not long,
    if I'm smart.

For holding on to a resentment
    is like swallowing poison
        and hoping the other
        person will die!

I must let it go —
    forgive and move on —
        for my own sake
        as well as theirs.

And I must remember
to let go of expectations, too,
    and love my friends
        just as they are —
            not how I expect them to be.

A True Friend...

Points out your good qualities when you forget.

A good friend is a connection to life –
a tie to the past, a road to the future,
the key to sanity in a totally insane world.

LOIS WYSE

MIRROR, MIRROR

Mirror, mirror on the wall,
    who's my best friend after all?

You are, dear one.

You show myself to myself
    when I am too blind to see.

You remind me who I am
and how I'm a wonderful person,
    when my self-esteem flags.

You point out my good qualities
    when all I notice are the bad ones.

You see,
    my problem is not that
    I'm a slow learner –
        it's that I'm a fast forgetter!

Fill in the Blanks

My mind is a mismatch detector.
I always notice what's wrong
 and overlook what's right.

My memory is faulty;
 my mirror is flawed.
I'm my own worst critic,
 seeing only my foibles and failings.

Then I hear your voice:

"I love the way you do that."

"You're so clever with these things."

"Gosh, I wish I was good at that, like you are."

"You're so_____ smart

        _____ creative

        _____ resourceful

        _____ (fill in the blank)

You remind me
    when I forget the good stuff.

Thanks, dear friend, I needed that!

A True Friend...

Questions you when you're about to do something really dumb.

A true friend never gets in your way, unless you happen to be going down.

ARNOLD GLASGOW

Second Opinion

"Are you sure you want to do that?"
    you ask me.
"What are your other options?"
    you query kindly.
"Would you like me to help you think this through?"
    you offer generously.
"Maybe you want to get another opinion,"
    you suggest supportively.

Some of my friends just go along to get along,
    saying "*yes*" to avoid conflict or hurt feelings.
But *true* friends, like you, ask courageous questions,
    speaking up when you're concerned for my well-being.

**Thank you for all the times
    you've saved me from myself!**

BLIND SPOTS

Help!
Stop me before
 I screw up again!

Why do I have
 these blind spots?
*Why don't I see
 these problems coming?*

You and Me friends forever

Thank goodness
    I have you to
        keep an eye out for me.

What was I thinking?!

Two heads really are better than one…
especially when one of those heads
    is yours.

A True Friend...

Respects your boundaries.

Across

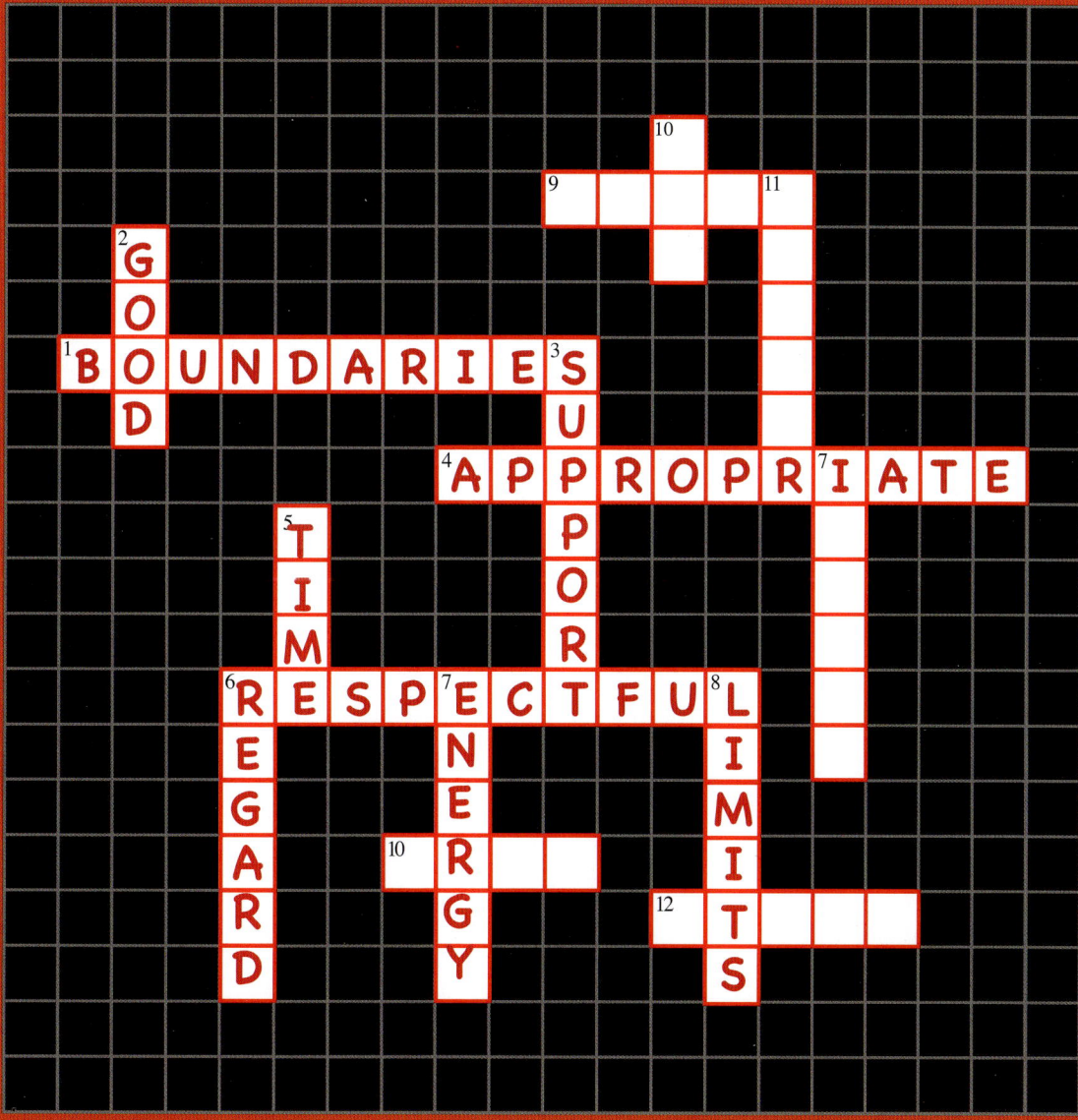

1. BOUNDARIES
4. APPROPRIATE
6. RESPECTFUL
9. (4 letters)
10. (4 letters)
12. (5 letters) ITS

Down

2. GOD
3. SUPPORT
5. TIME
6. REGARD
7. ENERGY
8. LIMITS
10. (2 letters)
11. (vertical)

LIMITS, NOT LIMITATIONS

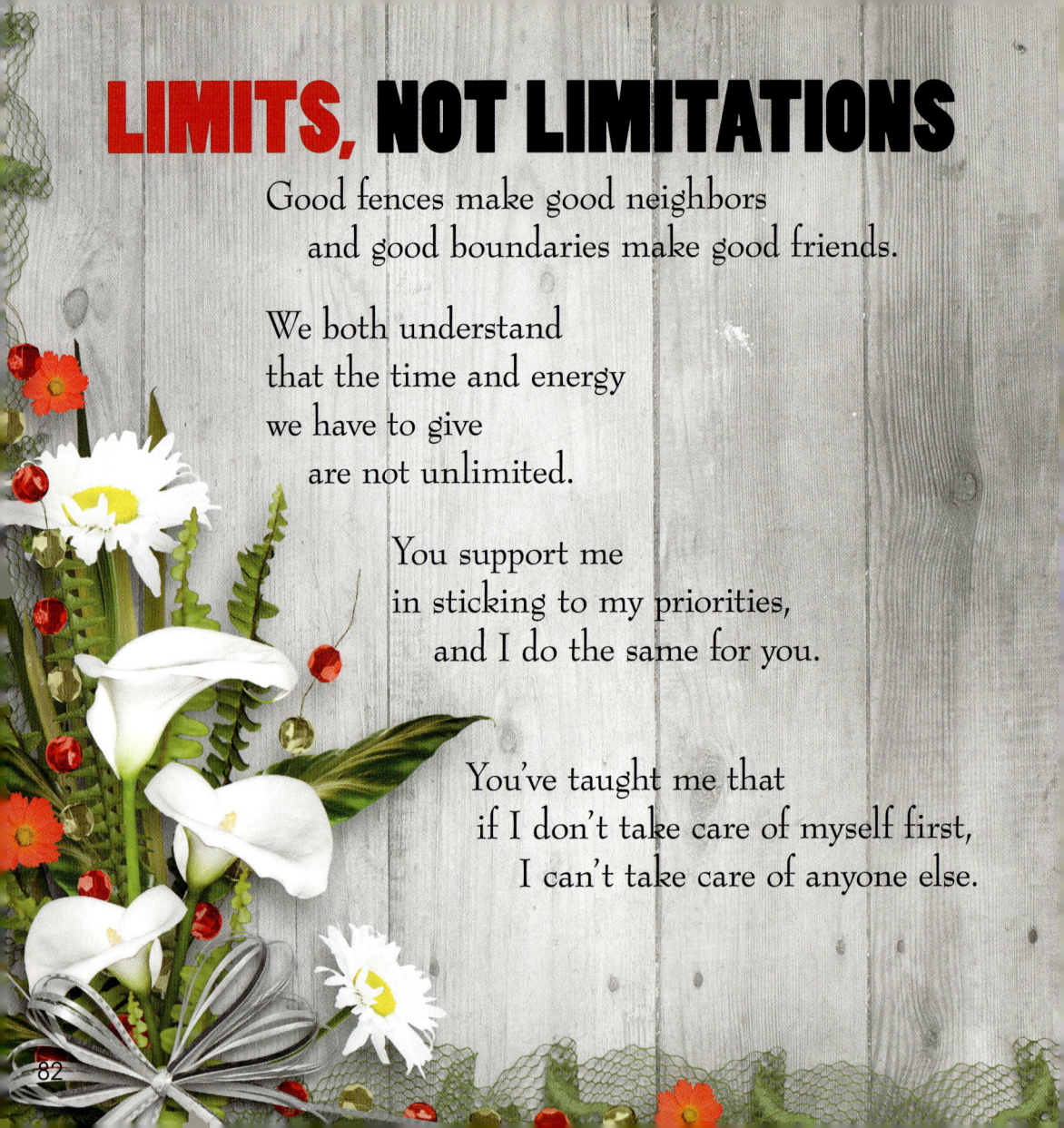

Good fences make good neighbors
   and good boundaries make good friends.

We both understand
that the time and energy
we have to give
   are not unlimited.

   You support me
   in sticking to my priorities,
     and I do the same for you.

   You've taught me that
     if I don't take care of myself first,
       I can't take care of anyone else.

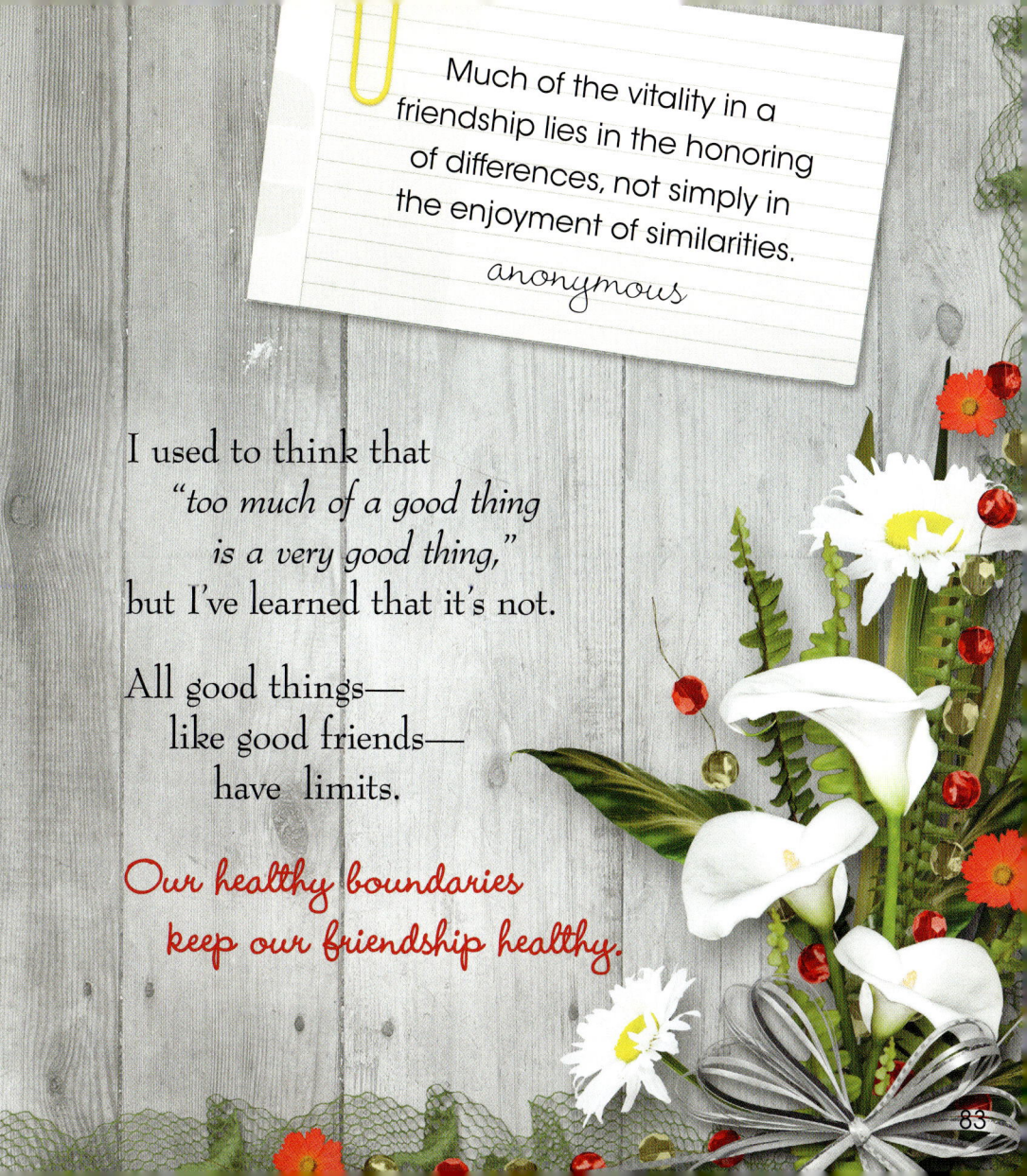

> Much of the vitality in a friendship lies in the honoring of differences, not simply in the enjoyment of similarities.
>
> *anonymous*

I used to think that
   "too much of a good thing
    is a very good thing,"
but I've learned that it's not.

All good things—
   like good friends—
     have limits.

Our healthy boundaries keep our friendship healthy.

The most beautiful discovery true friends make is that they can grow separately without growing apart.

ELISABETH FOLEY

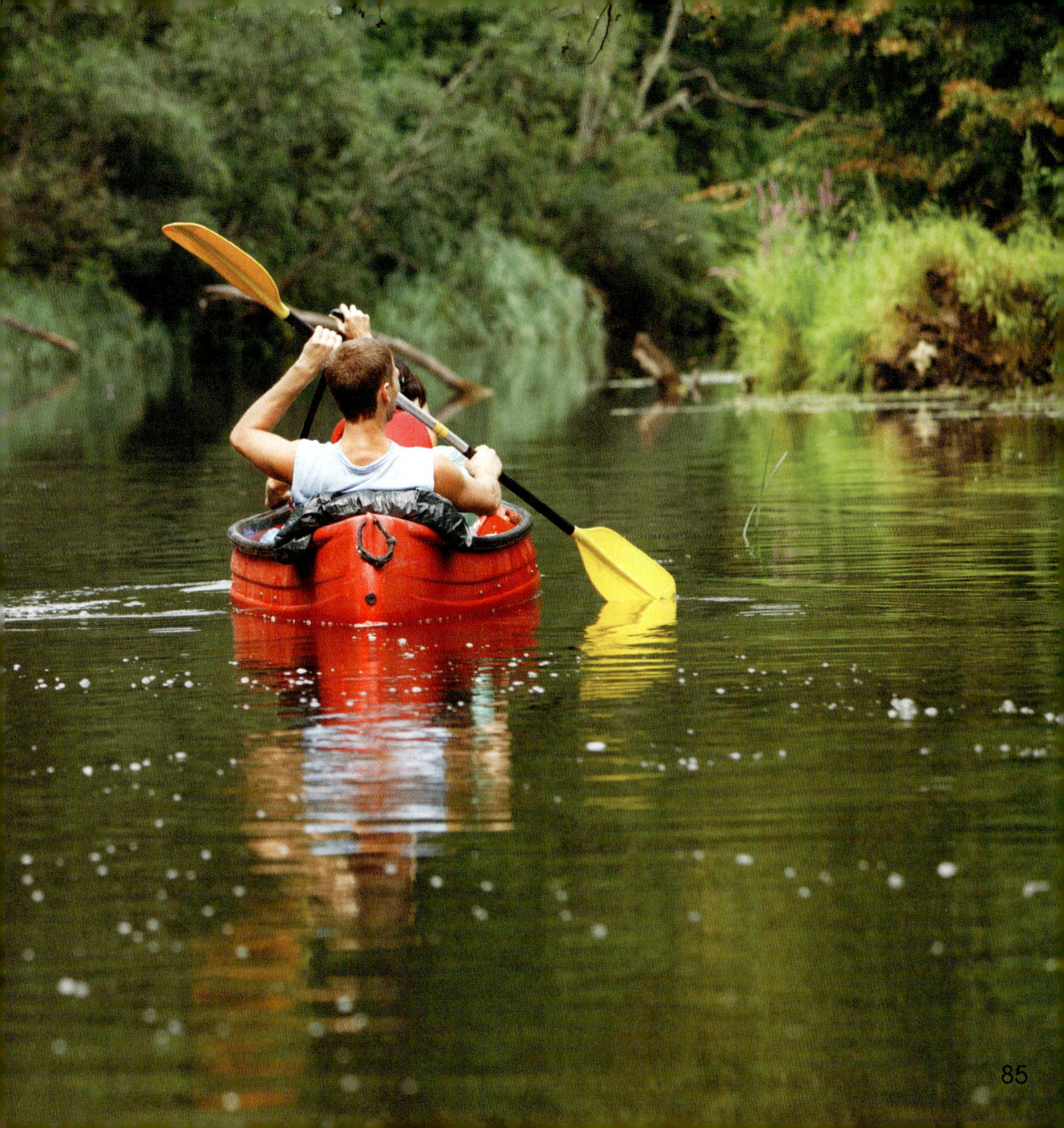

A True Friend...

Shares her hopes and fears with you.

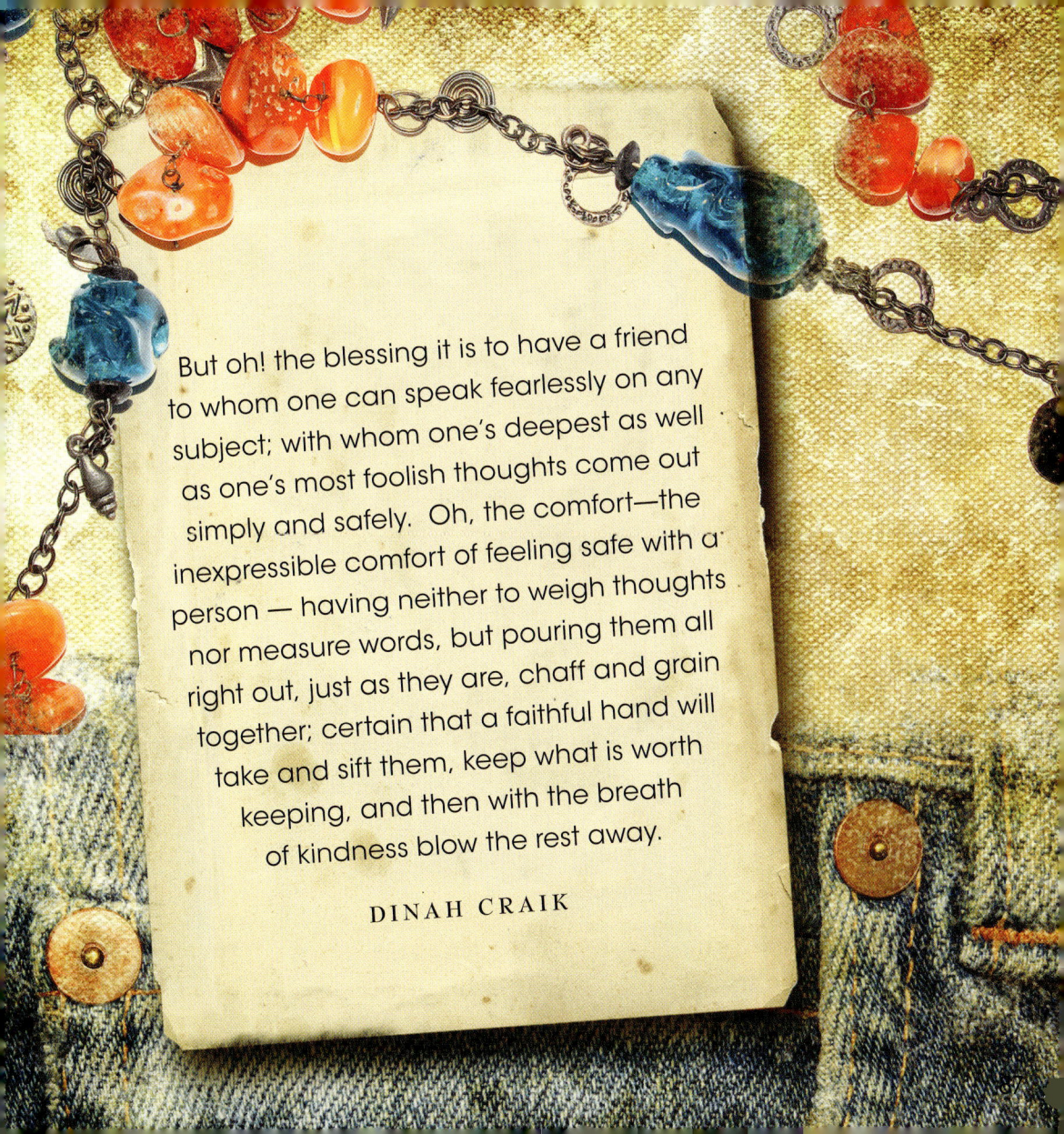

But oh! the blessing it is to have a friend to whom one can speak fearlessly on any subject; with whom one's deepest as well as one's most foolish thoughts come out simply and safely. Oh, the comfort—the inexpressible comfort of feeling safe with a person — having neither to weigh thoughts nor measure words, but pouring them all right out, just as they are, chaff and grain together; certain that a faithful hand will take and sift them, keep what is worth keeping, and then with the breath of kindness blow the rest away.

DINAH CRAIK

Recollections... Rock Collections

My heart is a jewel box
where I carefully stash
    the gems of hopes and dreams
      you share with me.
These beautiful baubles of hope
shine and sparkle
    in the light of possibility
when we look at them together.

Your fears are in there, too—
rough rocks that I wrap in velvet concern
    to keep them from scratching
      or damaging
        your bright hopes.

They're all in there together –
hopes and fears –
    coexisting side by side.

Hopes to be cherished,
fears to be respected –
  both true,
  both real,
  both valuable.
I keep them safe
    in the jewel box of my heart.

True friends remind you that **FEAR** is …

False
Evidence
Appearing
Real

A True Friend...

Tells you the truth.

A friend can tell you things you don't want to tell yourself.

FRANCES WARD WELLER

Mirror Image

My friends are mirrors.
They show me to myself.
They reflect what they see
   so that I can see it, too.

   The good
      the bad
         and the ugly.
   It's all there.

But their love enables me
   to see the truth
      through clear eyes,
without having to avert my gaze
   in shame or guilt.

Mirror, mirror on the wall,
   who's my best friend,
   after all?

Loving Truthteller

Experience has taught me that
  truth without love
  is simply brutality,
and
  love without truth
is just sentimentality.

It's both I need –
  truth with love –
and that's what you give me.

Thanks, dear friend,
  I needed that.

True Friends are
AUTHENTIC...

Aware

Understanding

Tactful

Honest

Empathetic

Natural

Tuned in

Intimate

Caring

A True Friend...

Understands you, even when you don't understand yourself.

True friendship is seen through the heart,
not through the eyes.

ANONYMOUS

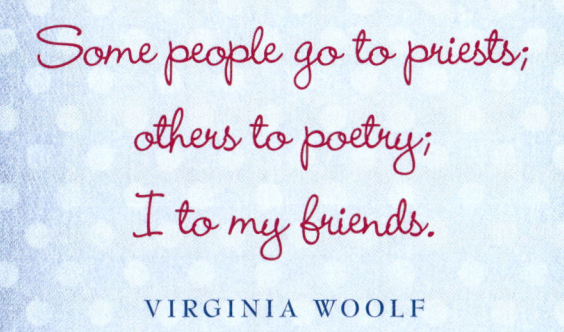

Some people go to priests;
others to poetry;
I to my friends.

VIRGINIA WOOLF

Friends are as companions on a journey, who ought to aid each other to persevere in the road to a happier life.

PYTHAGORAS

Ice Cream Hangover

"I can't believe it,"
   I groan,
"I ate a whole quart
of ice cream last night!
I'll never lose weight …
It's hopeless."

"It's not what you're eating—"
   you reply,
"It's what's eating you.
What was going on
before the ice cream?"

"I don't know …"
   I say.

"Why don't you spend some time
thinking and writing about it?"
   you suggest.

*"There's a message in the ice cream.
It's a gift.
What's it trying to tell you?"*

The gift of the ice cream …
    what a great way to think about it.

I love the way
    you help me
        understand myself.

IN THE FISHBOWL

Why is it that it's so easy to see
what someone else needs to do,
   when we can't see what we need to do?

The solutions to others' problems
seem blindingly obvious,
   while our own dilemmas befuddle us.

We're like fish in a fishbowl –
   we can't see the water
   because we're in it.

But others looking in from the outside
can see the water quite clearly.

Aren't I lucky
   to have friends like you –
     who see me and my life
     from a clear perspective?

You help me understand myself
   when my thinking
   (like a fishbowl)
   is cloudy.

You call me on my nonsense
   when I'm fooling myself.

You remind me that
   "denial" is not a river in Egypt.

I'm swimming safer in life
   thanks to your loving perspective.

A True Friend...

Values your ideas and opinions.

If instead of a gem, or even a flower, we should cast the gift of a loving thought into the heart of a friend, that would be giving as the angels give.

GEORGE MACDONALD

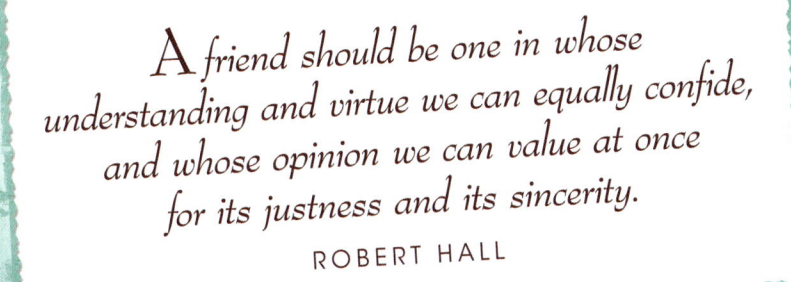

A friend should be one in whose understanding and virtue we can equally confide, and whose opinion we can value at once for its justness and its sincerity.

ROBERT HALL

The language of friendship is not words, but meanings.

HENRY DAVID THOREAU

Yours for the Asking

"What do you think?"
she asks,
and unlike some people
she really means it.

I value her counsel
and she mine.

We bounce ideas
back and forth
like so many tennis
balls.

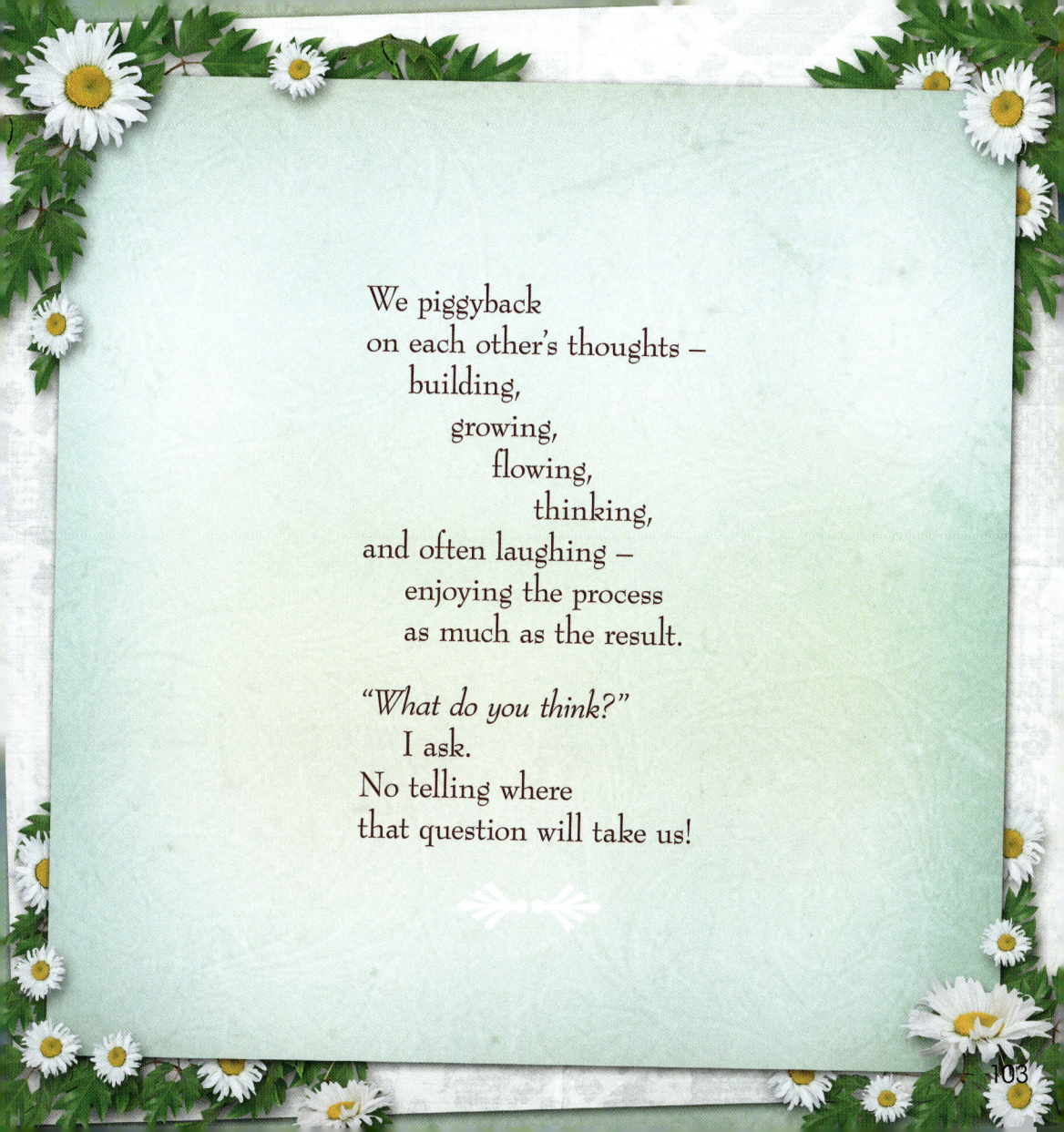

We piggyback
on each other's thoughts —
    building,
        growing,
            flowing,
                thinking,
and often laughing —
    enjoying the process
    as much as the result.

"What do you think?"
    I ask.
No telling where
that question will take us!

MINING FOR GOLD

All ideas
are not created equal.

Some are brilliant,
    others not so much.
And I hate to admit,
    but a few
    are even crazy!

As my friend
    you help me
        sort out my ideas –
separating the bright ones
from the dim,
    the inspired
    from the dull,
        the sublime
        from the ridiculous.

Your perspective is helpful,
your insight on target.

Thank you for helping me
find my 14K nuggets
amidst the Fool's Gold.

A True Friend...

Will do anything she can to help you.

It is not so much our friends' help that helps us, as the confidence of their help.

EPICURUS

Sweet Offering

"Is there anything I can do?"
    you ask.
What a sweet question.

Your heart,
your mind,
your schedule,
your home,
your pocketbook
    are always open to me
        if I need them.

Sometimes there's nothing
you can do…
    and we both know it.

But still you offer.
And in your offering
    I find everything I need.

Sometimes our light goes out but is blown into flame by another human being. Each of us owes deepest thanks to those who have rekindled this light.

› *Albert Schweitzer* ‹

If you light a lamp for somebody, it will also brighten your path.

› *Buddhist proverb* ‹

True Friends Offer a
HELPING HAND

Hearing what's needed
Eager to contribute
Listening with compassion
Paying attention to the little things
Intuitively understanding what's helpful and what's not
Never overstepping your bounds
Going out of your way for a true friend

Healing love, healing touch
Asking "What can I do to help?"
Never assuming that you know what's best
Desiring to serve and contribute to others' wellbeing

A True Friend...

Xtends the benefit of the doubt to you.

I always felt that the great high privilege, relief and comfort of friendship was that one had to explain nothing.

KATHERINE MANSFIELD

Doubtless

My friend is generous.
She always gives me
    the benefit of the doubt.

I forget to return her call sometimes.
I'm late for our lunch together.
I get lost on my way
    to our designated meeting place.

She doesn't chafe or pace –
    she knows I love her.
She tolerates my follies and foibles
    with patience and grace.
She knows my intentions are good,
    though sometimes there's a gap
        between intent and impact.

My friend is generous.
She always gives me
    the benefit of the doubt.

Never explain yourself.
Your friends don't need it
and your enemies
won't believe it.

Belgecia Howell

I'm treating you as a friend,
asking you to share my
present minuses in the hope
that I can ask you to share
my future pluses.

Katherine Mansfield

True friends enjoy
GIVING BACK...

Going the extra mile
Involved in each other's lives
Vested interest in mutual wellbeing
Interested in helping out
Needing one another
Growing by giving

Being gracious and kind
Acknowledging one another's love
Communicating lovingly, honestly
Keeping commitments to one another

A True Friend...

Yearns to hear from you when you're away.

I haven't seen you in a while, yet I often imagine all your expressions. I haven't spoke to you recently, but many times I hear your thoughts. Good friends must not always be together. It is the feeling of oneness when distant that proves a lasting.

ANONYMOUS

Absence makes our friendship fonder

Time goes by …
Friends come and go
    just as the seasons do.
But true friends come and never go,
    though time and distance
      may sometimes
        keep us apart.

I miss you when you're away.
My days are busy and full, as usual,
but still …
    something's missing.

I long to hear your voice on the phone,
    or see your face as you walk through my door.

For when we connect,
    time and distance seem to melt away.
We pick up right where we left off …
    and it's as if you were never gone at all.

Absence makes our friendship stronger.

If ever there is tomorrow when we're not together, there is something you must always remember: You're braver than you believe, stronger than you seem, and smarter than you think. But the most important thing is, even if we're apart, I'll always be with you.

Christopher Robin to Pooh

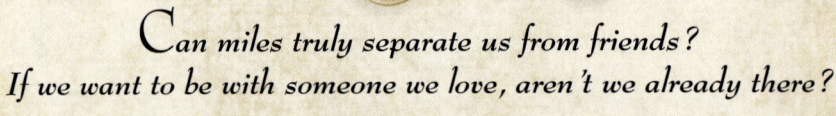

Can miles truly separate us from friends? If we want to be with someone we love, aren't we already there?

Richard Bach

Sometimes, when you're far away,
I find myself ...

Listening for the phone.
Opening my mailbox eagerly each afternoon.
Noticing how much I miss you.
Going about my day wondering how your day is going.

Delighting in your postcards and e-mail from afar.
Interested in your adventures.
Seeing a movie and thinking how much you'd like it.
Taking time to note things I want to tell you about.
Anticipating the catching up we'll do when you come home.
Never going to bed without saying a prayer for you.
Counting the days.
Eagerly awaiting your return.

A True Friend...

Zings with joy 'cause you're friends.

If friends were flowers, I'd pick you.

ANONYMOUS

What do you mean to me,
TRUE FRIENDS?

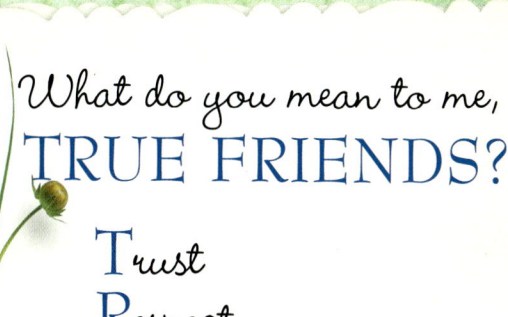

Trust
Respect
Understanding
Empathy

Forgiveness
Responsiveness
Insight
Expressions of love
Needing one another
Dependability
Spiritual connection

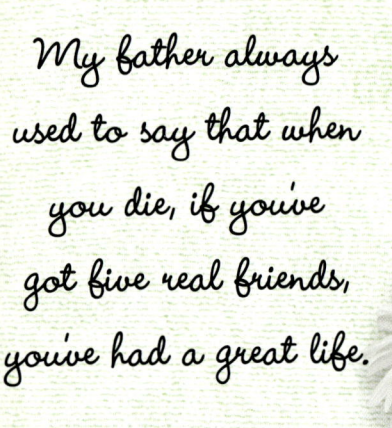

My father always used to say that when you die, if you've got five real friends, you've had a great life.

LEE IACOCCA

A single rose can be my garden ... a single friend, my world.

LEO BUSCAGLIA

Kindred Spirits

Who knows why
    I love being with you?
Is it your energy?
    Your curiosity?
    Your sense of humor?
    Your talent and creativity?
Yes, all of the above.
I love the way we connect —
    we just click.

I can tell you feel the same about me —
    I can just feel it.
A mutual admiration society,
    that's what we have.
Why is it special with you
    and not with someone else?

I don't know —
    don't have to.
I just accept the joy
    for what it is ...
        gratefully.

THE FRIENDSHIP PROMISE©

BY BJ GALLAGHER

I believe that true friends accept each other just as they are,
    and I promise to love you unconditionally.

I believe that true friends listen with their hearts as well as their ears,
    and I promise to give you my attention and affection.

I believe that true friends keep each other's confidences,
    and I promise to be trustworthy and loyal.

I believe that true friends complement each other,
    and I promise to celebrate our uniqueness and similarities.

I believe that true friends compliment each other,
    and I promise to acknowledge your many wonderful qualities –
        especially when you forget.

I believe that true friends enjoy a sense of humor,
    and I promise to laugh with you, not at you.

I believe that true friends rely on each other in good times and bad,
    and I promise to be there for you.

I believe that true friends are honest with each other,
    and I promise to tell you the truth with love.

I believe that true friends forgive each other's mistakes and failings,
    and I promise to let go of disappointments and resentments.

I believe that true friends share generously,
    and I promise to open my heart and my home to you.

I believe that true friends love spending time together,
    and I promise to make time for you.

I believe that true friends cherish each other,
and I promise to honor your feelings.

I believe that true friends allow each other the dignity of their own choices,
    and I promise to respect and support you in your decisions.

I believe that true friends give each other the freedom to be who they are,
    and I promise to love you for being *you*.

© 2011 BJ Gallagher

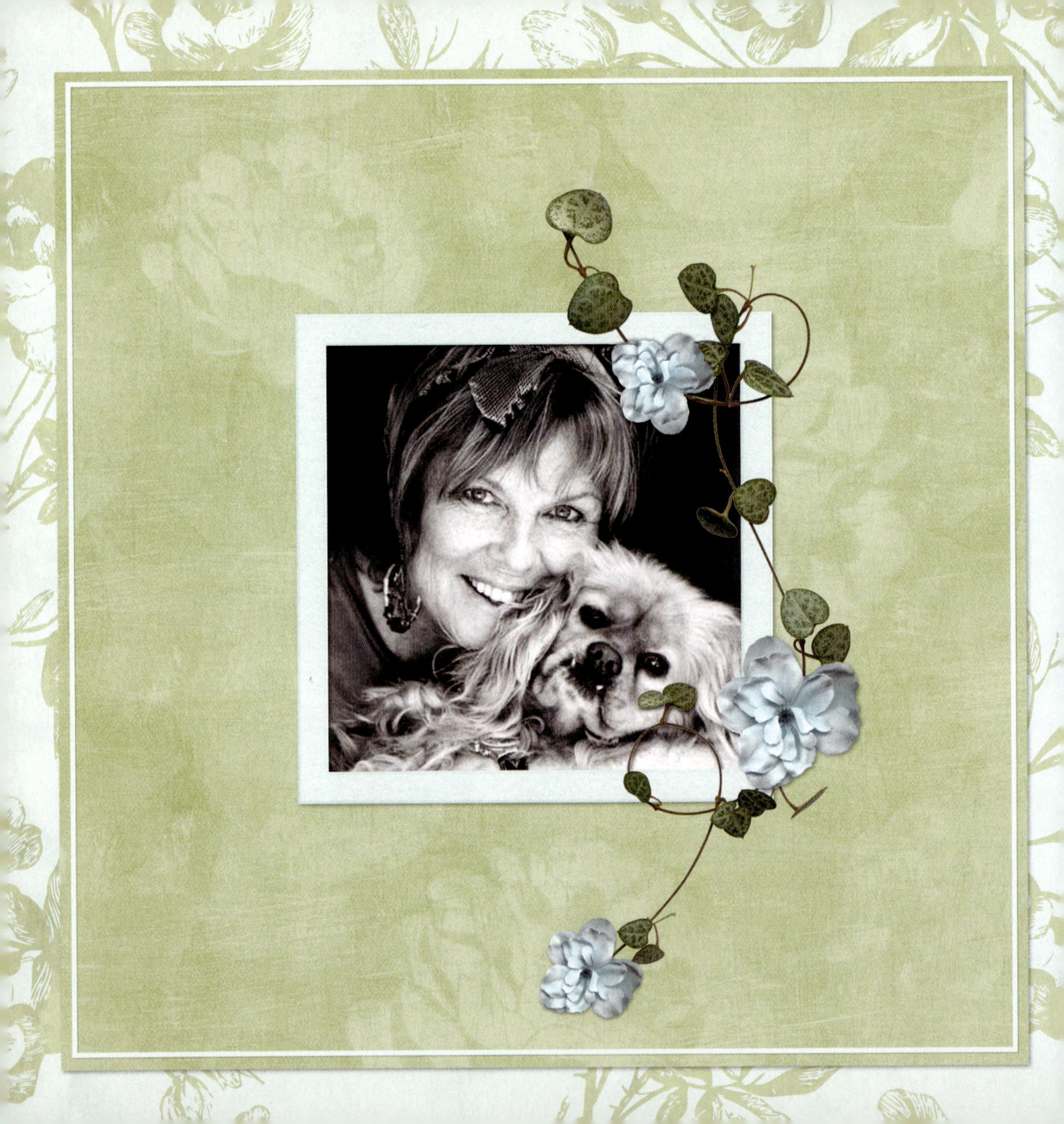

BJ Gallagher

BJ Gallagher is an author, speaker, story-teller, and poet. Poetry is the language of the heart, and the heart is where we hold our friends — like precious gems in a jewel box.

BJ has written twenty-five books, including the international best-seller, *A Peacock in the Land of Penguins* (now published in 23 languages). She is also the author or coauthor of several popular Simple Truths books:

- *Learning to Dance in the Rain:* The Power of Gratitude
- *The Best Way Out is Always Through:* The Power of Perseverance
- *Oil for Your Lamp:* Women Taking Care of Themselves
- *Oh, Thank Goodness, It's Not Just Me!:* Woman to Woman, Heart to Heart
- *The Road to Happiness:* Simple Secrets for a Happy Life

BJ lives in her cozy cottage in Los Angeles with some of her favorite friends — the four-legged, furry variety.

Visit her web site: www.bjgallagher.com

Oh, Thank Goodness,
Oil for Your Lamp
Women Taking Care of Themselves
LISA HAMMOND & BJ GALLAGHER

simple truths®
Motivational & Inspirational Gifts

If you have enjoyed this book we invite you to check out our entire collection of gift books, with free inspirational movies, at www.simpletruths.com.
You'll discover it's a great way to inspire friends and family, or to thank your best customers and employees.

For more information, please visit us at:
WWW.SIMPLETRUTHS.COM

OR CALL US TOLL FREE...
800-900-3427